TIMELESS VENICE

TIMELESS
VENICE

Sandra Forty

CHARTWELL
BOOKS, INC.

This edition published in 2007 by

CHARTWELL BOOKS, INC.
A Division of
BOOK SALES, INC.
114 Northfield Avenue
Edison, New Jersey 08837

ISBN-13: 978-0-7858-2316-2
ISBN-10: 0-7858-2316-6

© 2007 Compendium Publishing, 43 Frith Street,
London, Soho, W1V 4SA, United Kingdom

Cataloging-in-Publication data is available from the
Library of Congress

Printed and bound in China

Design: Compendium Design

PAGE 2: The island and church of San Giorgio Maggiore
dominated by its impressive campanile looks out over St.
Mark's Basin.

PAGE 4: The Grand Canal sweeps through Venice in a
dramatic reverse S-shape. This is at the station end
looking toward the Church of Saint Geremia whose
dome is visible alongside the Fondamenta Labia, one
of Venice's oldest campaniles.

Contents

Introduction   6

Early Years   18

The Golden Age   44

Decline and end of the Republic   70

Modern Venice   98

Index and Credits   160

Introduction

Timeless Venice—gondolas in front of San Giorgio Maggiore.

Introduction

Venice, or more properly Venezia, is a major seaport and capital of the province of Venezia and the region of Veneto. The city itself sits in an archipelago of about 118 original islands almost at the heart of its crescent-shaped 212 square mile Lagoon that stretches from northeast to southwest for about 32 miles. The Lagoon is sheltered from the ravages of the Adriatic Sea by a sandbar known as the Lido. The famous Grand Canal follows the course of the original main stream of the River Brenta, and many of the other canals also follow the old water courses between the islands.

Venice was once one of the most important and powerful trading and political powers in the entire Mediterranean area. This very wealth and importance was ultimately to prove to be Venice's downfall as the city's wealth attracted greedy predators, not least Napoleon Bonaparte who was personally responsible for setting the city's decline in motion.

During the Renaissance Venice was one of the great shining centers of artistic creativity, and during this period many of the city's magnificent palaces and churches were built. For centuries wealthy beyond dreams, Venice suffered a long period of decline and occupation by unsympathetic invaders, and almost in sympathy it seems, the city started to sink back into the Lagoon and the grand buildings started their inexorable decay. But Venice's beauty, even in splendid decay, came to its rescue and has attracted not only artists and poets but also tourists by the thousand. One of the "must see" destinations of the nineteenth century Grand Tour, Venice these days has become one of the premier tourist destinations on the planet, and the entire city became a designated UNESCO World Heritage area in 1987.

Venice's Lagoon was created by the River Po delta at the northwest end of the Adriatic, a northern offshoot of the Mediterranean Sea. For much of its illustrious history Venice was a separate state from the rest of mainland Italy with its own distinctive history, traditions, customs, and way of life. Venice is

ABOVE: The dark red and gold flag of "La Serenissima"—the Republic of Venice—features the winged lion, the symbol of St. Mark the Evangelist, patron saint of the city.

RIGHT: Maps of modern Venice and the growth of the Venetian empire.

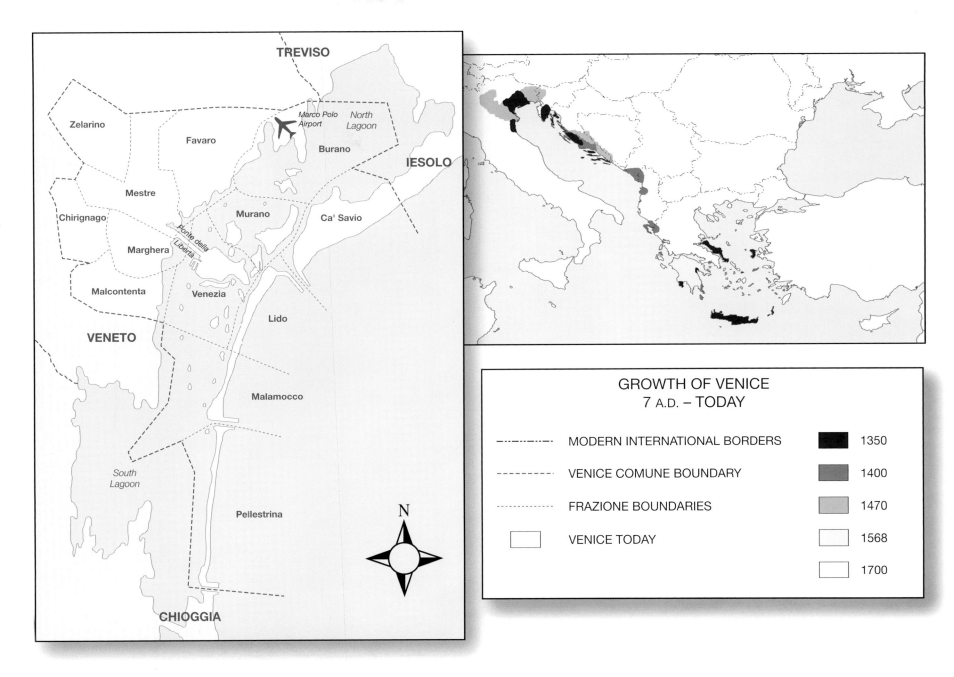

TREVISO

Zelarino

Favaro

Marco Polo
Airport

North
Lagoon

Burano

IESOLO

Mestre

Chirignago

Murano

Ca' Savio

Ponte della
Libertà

Marghera

Venezia

Malcontenta

Lido

VENETO

Malamocco

South
Lagoon

Pellestrina

N

CHIOGGIA

GROWTH OF VENICE
7 A.D. – TODAY

── · ── · ──	MODERN INTERNATIONAL BORDERS	■ 1350
── ── ──	VENICE COMUNE BOUNDARY	▨ 1400
··········	FRAZIONE BOUNDARIES	▤ 1470
☐	VENICE TODAY	☐ 1568
		☐ 1700

9

built on ancient wooden pilings, and due to a number of reasons slowly sank almost four inches during the 20th century. The sinkage was mostly due to industrial groundwater extraction which has virtually stopped since the 1960s when the artesian wells on the mainland were capped. The city currently sinks by up to a millimeter a year as the subsoil is compacted under the weight of the buildings and eroded by the movement of the waters. A more pertinent threat is the rising sea level caused by global warming and the melting of the Arctic icecap.

Venice is particularly vulnerable every six months between early October and April—especially during October, November, and December—when unusually high tides can pour *acque alte*, or "high water," into the city. The official definition of an acque alte event is when the tide is 3.54 inches above normal high tide. The occurrence of an acque alte requires three simultaneous natural occurrences: a combination of low atmospheric pressure from the north that blows in a cold wind from the Hungarian steppes known as the bora; at the same time, high atmospheric pressure pulls in the hot sirocco winds from Syria blowing northward up the narrow and comparatively shallow Adriatic Sea, which forces water up and into the Venetian Lagoon. The full, and sometimes the new, moon causes the highest tides which build even higher when the bora and sirocco winds whip up the waves of the Adriatic to dangerous heights. These crash through the three entrances to Venice and flood the city, as happened so disastrously in 1966. Every twenty years or so the winds combine to raise the tide by about three feet, and every 200 years by a catastrophic five feet. The next massive inundation is scheduled for 2030 but it is hoped that sufficient defenses will be in place to prevent disaster.

St. Mark's Square is the lowest point in Venice and is flooded well over forty times a year—in the 1920s it flooded on average around ten times a year. In the 20th century the relative sea level in Venice has increased by over nine

RIGHT: Rising water rippling over the streets of Venice has become an increasingly common sight. When the Lagoon rises and floods into the city the event is known locally as an "acque alte" or high water. The acque alte becomes official when the tide is 3.54 inches above normal high tide.

inches due to a combination of rising sea levels and sinking land. To make matters worse the surrounding Lagoon is suffering from severe environmental degradation from agricultural, industrial, and urban pollution which has caused colossal water quality problems.

Perhaps the greatest glory of Venice is the magnificent architecture evident all around the old city. There are some 450 palaces and important building around the canals all built in a mixture of styles: Italian, Arabic, Byzantine, Gothic, Renaissance, Mannerist, and Baroque. The early Venetian builders and architects had to improvise to construct their buildings on the low lying mud banks and islands by using wooden piles driven as deep as possible into the silt and mud or built on top of stone infill. On top of the wooden piles the builders placed wooden layers, followed by brick courses and then stone.

LEFT, RIGHT, AND BELLOW: Unmistakable Venice: St. Mark's, winged lions, and gondolas—all part of Venice's characteristic magic.

13

Saint Mark

The symbol of the city of Venice is the winged lion holding an open book in its paw: this is also the symbol of St. Mark, the patron saint of Venice. St. Mark the Evangelist is the author of St. Mark's Gospel and was originally from Jerusalem. Legend says that he traveled to Rome and Alexandria preaching the word of Christ and was probably martyred in the Church of Alexandria. In 829 his relics were stolen by two merchants from Torcello, who the story goes, hid the relics under some pork so the Muslim soldiers and officials would not look too closely. The relics were taken back to Venice where they were greeted with great celebrations and (originally) placed in a shrine in the church of San Marco. His saint's day is April 25.

RIGHT: The distinctive prow of a gondola silhouetted against the waters.

FAR RIGHT: Gondolas are by law painted black and propeled by a single oar or rèmo.

BELOW: A statue of the iconic winged lion of St. Mark stands proudly in front of St. Mark's Basilica.

PAGES 16–17: A procession over a temporary bridge on the Grand Canal (LEFT) and St. Mark's Square at night (RIGHT).

Early Years

Early Years

In the 1st century B.C. the location that was to become Venice was an administrative region of the Roman Empire called Venetia. It comprised the Veneto, Friuli, and Trentino areas, and while it is quite possible that the Romans established a port in Venice, there is no archaeological evidence to prove it. In 330 A.D. the capital of the Roman Empire was transferred to Byzantium and the Veneto became a province of Byzantium. In 452 A.D. Attila the Hun invaded northern Italy and the population of the countryside fled for their lives to the small islands peppering the lagoons of the western coast of the Adriatic. When Attila's armies withdrew, many refugees returned to their mainland homes but it is thought that many stayed on islands such as Torcello, Burano, and Malamocco, and so started the settlement that grew up to become Venice.

Despite being a Byzantine protectorate, the peoples living around the floodplains of the River Po enjoyed little protection from their overseers and were constantly harassed in the 6th and 7th centuries by the Lombards encroaching on their lands from the north. Slowly but steadily the populations were driven back toward the coast and into the swampy marshlands and islands of the Po delta where the beginnings of Venice were set up.

By the 7th century Venice was sufficiently established and ordered to start electing its own governor—the Doge—with the sanction of Byzantium. When the Franks led by Pepin, the son of Charlemagne, invaded in 810 they easily overwhelmed the mainland towns but were unable to get across the tidal channel to reach their principal target, the island of Malamocco, the Venetian

VIAGGIO DA VENETIA

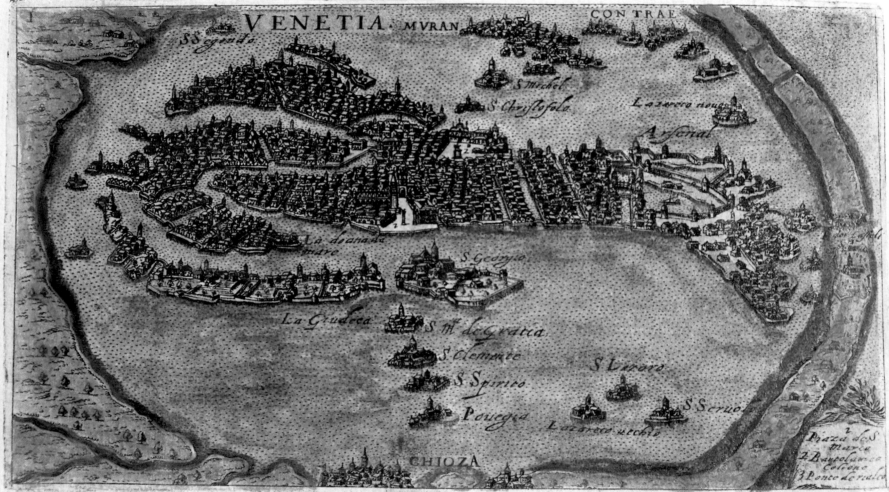

LEFT AND ABOVE: Due to its trading importance and influential mercantile fleet Venice was mapped from the earliest times. The maps were often more beautiful than informative and embellished with fanciful sea monsters and gods of the seas.

capital. The Byzantine fleet was despatched to protect the settlements, and when a peace pact was eventually reached Venice and the surrounding Lagoon was confirmed as belonging to the Byzantine Empire. Nevertheless the Franks remained a constant threat and the inhabitants of the lagoon decided that for their own safety they would do better moving to the more isolated and protected islands in the center of the lagoon. This land was known as Rivo Alto (also Ri'Alto) meaning "high bank" as the islands were made up of sedimentary deposits from the Brenta River delta, whose mouth lay several miles to the west.

As the settlement grew the inhabitants edged outward into the Lagoon from the central islands and mudbanks by constructing ridges of wooden pilings and landfilling in behind them. In 827 the Veneto area came under the jurisdiction of the Aquileia as the Franks yet again threatened to invade. The mood however changed the following year when two merchants made a remarkable coup by acquiring the relics of St. Mark and took them home to Venice—the enthusiasm and delight of the people gave them a taste for freedom from foreign overseers and Venetians quickly declared religious and political independence from outside authorities. The winged lion of St. Mark was adopted as the symbol of their new state and a political structure for government was begun. By the 10th century the city of Venice had the basis of its political structures and foundation for mercantile fortune.

Venetian merchants and traders were already important members of the Adriatic and Mediterranean economy and their wealth went back to Venice providing the city with increasingly greater trading and economic muscle. Goods and produce were brought into Venice, warehoused there, and then sold on. With each transaction Venetians cut a profit and soon Venice was the economic balance of their former masters in Byzantium, and was able to

FAR LEFT: The Arsenal photographed in the last decade of the 19th century. The first arsenal was probably constructed around 1104 and was instrumental in ensuring Venice's naval and maritime power.

LEFT: An early photograph of the interior of St. Mark's Basilica showing the elaborate religious church furniture and impressive wall mosaics.

negotiate a favorable alliance on equal terms. In return for Venetian support against Islam and the voracious Normans (who controlled Sicily among other lands) Byzantium granted commercial privileges to Venice in the Orient.

Other maritime republics such as Pisa and Genoa were trading rivals but no real match for the feared Venetians whose wealth and war galleys dominated the Adriatic, as well as much of the eastern Mediterranean. Venice's wealth increased even more with the Crusades, when ships, food, supplies, and money flooded to and from the city, with the Venetian merchants getting wealthier at every exchange. Venetian traders and merchants became the power brokers all around the Mediterranean. By the 12th century Venice was a maritime and trading power to be reckoned with, so much so that in 1177 Venice had sufficient prestige to be able to broker the peace treaty between the Holy Roman Emperor Frederick Barbarossa and Pope Alexander III—the two most powerful and significant figures in Europe.

In 1201 Pope Innocent III sent out the Fourth Crusade to conquer Jerusalem after invading Egypt. But proceedings turned into farce as plans and plots changed the direction of the crusade. To get the 33,500 troops to Egypt the leader of the Crusade, Count Boniface of Montferrat, did a deal with Doge Enrico Dandolo to use Venetian transport. But when only 12,000 Crusaders arrived in Venice, the Count could not raise the agreed sum (much to the Doge's fury), so instead it was decided that the financial shortfall could be recouped in Byzantium (Constantinople) if the Crusaders helped the deposed Byzantine emperor's son, Aslexius, recapture the throne. Accordingly in 1204, the Crusaders lay siege to Byzantium. The city fell on April 12 and was viciously sacked and the hapless inhabitants put to the sword. The Latin Empire of Constantinople was established and Venice was apportioned large

RIGHT AND FAR RIGHT: The Tetrarchs—the four leaders—a porphyry sculpture taken from a palace in 1204 during the sack of Byzantium, looted and brought back to Venice and now situated on the surviving corner tower of the original Doge's Palace. The carvings are Egyptian-Syrian and date from the 4th century and are reputed to portray Diocletian and the other three Emperors who reigned with him.

parts of the empire and most of the commercial privileges. Huge amounts of looted booty made their way back to Venice including the magnificent gilded statues of four horses that now prance on the top of St. Mark's basilica; although the ones there today are replicas, as the originals are now safely undercover.

The deposed Byzantine emperors now allied with Venice's Italian trading rival Genoa and reconquered the Eastern Empire in 1261. Venice immediately lost virtually all of the commercial privileges it had gained after the fall of Byzantium, as well as some of the lands. An uneasy truce was established which lasted between 1270-90. The commercial struggle with Genoa was resumed until 1299 when another peace was agreed.

Throughout the 13th and 14th centuries the mercantile trading city-states of Pisa, Genoa, and Venice were continually contesting a long series of conflicts for the control of Mediterranean and Levantine trade. This climaxed on September 9, 1298, when the Venetian and Genoan fleets met in battle near the island of Curzola, off the coast of southern Dalmatia. The Venetian fleet was led by Admiral Andrea Dandolo, the son of the Doge Giovanni Dandolo. The Venetians lost heavily, including the life of Admiral Dandolo, but managed to obtain reasonable peace conditions. The story also goes that the legendary Venetian explorer Marco Polo (1254–1324) was at the battle, fighting on the Venetian side and was captured and imprisoned for a time by the Genoans, during which time he dictated his memoires—*Il Milione* (called in English *The Travels of Marco Polo*).

Venice nevertheless remained prosperous and many of her citizens became very wealthy through trade, especially with the East. Venice warehoused and prepared goods before selling them on or trading them further into mainland Europe. This led to an unprecedented upheaval in the Venetian social structure as newly wealthy merchants wanted to assert their political muscle in Venetian politics, much to the dismay of the Venetian patricians. Additionally, the Doge became as much a liability as an advantage depending on his personal abilities, his immense power allowed him so much leeway that he was in effect uncontrollable.

In 1334 the Black Death destroyed around two-thirds of the population of China and in the following years the plague started to move westward. The plague reached Europe, in particular Venice, in 1348 via fleas living on the black rats hiding among the spice and silk cargoes of the merchant trading vessels. The disease was devastating as Venice rapidly lost as much as half her population which in turn led to a serious economic crisis, during which time of weakness Ludwig I of Hungary took the opportunity to annexe Dalmatia for himself. Similarly rival traders, in particular from Milan, Padua, and Ferrara seriously threatened Venetian trading interests and trading rivalry intensified all over the Adriatic and eastern Mediterranean.

In 1379 the Genoan fleet managed to penetrate the Ventian Lagoon and seized the island of Chioggia. The Venetians immediately counterattacked and managed to conclude a peace treaty in 1381 at Turin, however, Genoa although generously served in the treaty, was too drained by the expense of the conflict and too internally riven to ever pose a serious threat to Venice again. Venetian trade was now almost unchallenged and she extended her empire across the Mediterranean. Venice cultivated and operated an impressive and extensive diplomatic network and maintained a remarkably neutral diplomatic position between the great powers of Europe. The Republic was primarily interested in protecting and promoting her trading position and the access and prerogatives that her merchants enjoyed in trading locations across much of the known world. It was not in Venice's financial and trading interests to take sides in the many European conflicts of the period: instead they sought to supply both sides with goods and services whenever possible.

In 1384 the Ottoman Empire opened an embassy in Venice and promises of peace and friendship were made between the two most important Mediterranean powers. Indeed when the following treaty of 1406 allowed Venetians to move freely around the empire without being charged the extra

LEFT: Old carvings such as this plaque of winged griffins decorate many of the buildings around the older parts of Venice.

taxes they would otherwise incur as merchants, it seemed that Venice had established a platform for even greater wealth and prestige. As far as Venice was concerned the Ottoman threat was postponed but trouble started in March 1416 when the Ottoman Empire suddenly devastated the Venetian holdings of Eubea and Cicladi.

Elsewhere the Republic fared better: before 1405 the only part of the Italian mainland controlled by Venice was Treviso, Belluno, and Feltre. But by 1389 Venetian mercenary armies had taken Padua, Vicenza, and Verona. Then by 1420 they added Friuli and retook Dalmatia to make it once again Venetian. Eight years later Venice added the lands of Brescia and Bergamo giving the Republic in the process control over much of Lombardy. All these acquisitions were ratified by the Peace of Lodi in 1454 and then added to include Cremona and Polesine di Rovigo. Venice now controlled all the north bank of the Po from Ferrara to the Adriatic. But along with these new lands Venice also gathered new enemies, especially when the Republic took advantage of the warring political situation elsewhere in Italy to occupy the papal ports of Ravenna and Faenza and the Neapolitan ports of Bari and Brindisi.

LEFT: Tall cypress trees loom behind the wall that runs around the Cemetery and Monastery of San Michele on the Isle of the Dead. The cemetery is full and Venetians now have to be buried on the mainland.

ABOVE LEFT: A stone angel from the cemetery.

ABOVE: The church and monastery of San Michele were built between 1469 and 1535.

LEFT: The 24-hour clock and campanile of San Giacomo di Rialto. This tiny church is the oldest in Venice and shaped in the form of a Greek cross. The original church was probably founded in the 5th century but this building dates from sometime between the 11th and 12th centuries.

ABOVE: The Doge's Palace from an old postcard dating around 1890. The view is from La Giudecca, the long island south of the main city. The beautiful carved 14th century loggia dominates the facade of the palace and is nearly 500 feet long. It was designed by Giovanni Buon and built between 1309 and 1424.

ABOVE, RIGHT, AND FAR RIGHT: Venice is a wonderful place for those interested in early European architecture—particularly that of the 15th and 16th centuries. Ornate loggias can be seen in the palazzos of the rich all over the city, the columns surmounted by the quatrefoil tracery so often to be found in Gothic and Renaissance architecture. These damaged columns are preserved in the Doge's Palace.

LEFT: The Horses of St Mark's—the Quadriga—were plundered from the top of the Hippodrome in Byzantium (Constantinople) by Venetians in 1204 following the sack of the city during the Fourth Crusade. Byzantium had for centuries been the master of Venice, so the sack was partially ancient revenge for long years of subservience. The then Doge, Enrico Dandolo, while a young man had worked in Byzantium as an ambassador during which time he developed a deep hatred for the city. He was one of the principal leaders of the Fourth Crusade and personally directed much of the looting of the city. The horses are cast from a particularly unusual form of copper and were possibly Roman in origin. Each horse was cast in two sections, a head and body, with the join hidden by the collar. Some consider that the slightly awkward angle of the heads proves that they were brought back from Byzantium in two pieces and arbitrarily reassembled.

FAR LEFT: Venice's ships ferried goods all round the Mediterranean. Unsurprisingly, control of customs was of prime importance and so it is that Venice's Sea Customs Point—the Dogana di Mare—is at the entrance to the Grand Canal. In the late 17th century the original 14th-century tower was replaced by the classical colonnaded building seen here.

The Doge

The Doge was elected via a labyrinthine selection and voting process from one of the patrician Venetian families, and then held the position for life, although only for a minimal salary. In theory the Doge was the oldest and shrewdest Venetian. He had to abide by strict rules and regulations which were structured to minimize the leeway for corruption as he simultaneously became the ecclesiastical, civil, and the military leader of Venice.

A Doge was not allowed to give privileges to members of his family and was not allowed to name his suc-

RIGHT AND FAR RIGHT: The most beautiful clock in Venice sits facing the sea on the main facade of the gateway between St Mark's Square and the Merceria. The clock face shows the signs of the zodiac and the planets against a dark blue, star-studded background, as well as the hours, months, and phases of the sun and moon. All these elements provided essential information to Venice's sailors and merchants whose affluence, living, and maritime safety depended so much on the sea and the seasons.

cessor (although a few tried). He did, however, remain actively involved in trade, the lifeblood of Venice. When the Doge died a commission of inquisori investigated his tenure and passed judgement on his actions with the possibility of fining his estate for any mistakes: this was the only serious curb to his behavior.

Internal Venetian rivalries were dangerous to Venetian prosperity as a whole and although various Councils of Sages were established to control the power of the Doge and elements were put in place to monitor his election it was more important that Venice present a unified front in the constant fights with Constantinople and Genoa in the cutthroat trading wars. Accordingly, in 1297 the Grand Council was "closed"—an event known as the Serrata—and only members of Venice's two hundred or so patrician families recorded in the Libra D'Oro, (Golden Book) could take part in government and qualified as a possible Doge.

The Libra D'Oro contained the records of births, deaths, and marriages of all the noble Venetian families, now only they could vote or hold office. Membership of the governing council was automatic and for life, and a member's responsibility was to sit for limited periods on one of the various councils. The 200-strong Senate formed government policy, the College ran government business and saw to it that decisions were acted upon and laws upheld, and the Council of Ten was responsible for state security. All of them were answerable to the Doge.

RIGHT: The Doge's Palace and the Columns of St. Mark's from an 1890s' postcard. Venice was one of the first great vacation destinations in the very earliest days of tourism attracting people from all over the developed world.

FAR RIGHT: Interior courtyard of the Doge's Palace. Although a building of business and government the palace is a magnificent

work of art in itself and is one of the finest examples of Gothic art anywhere.

FOLLOWING PAGE, LEFT: The five-domed rooftop of St. Mark's Basilica.

FOLLOWING PAGE, RIGHT: The Doge's Palace showing the original position of the bronze Horses of St. Mark's (now replicas) on the Loggia dei Cavalli.

S. MARCO

ABOVE, RIGHT, AND FAR RIGHT: Differing
views of St Mark's Basilica, properly called
San Marco in Italian. The building was
originally built in 1094 and based on two
Byzantine basilicas (St. Sophia being one)
and is built with a centralized Greek cross
floorplan. It was continuously embellished
and improved over the following centuries
as Venetian wealth and importance
increased. Some of the ornamentation was
Oriental loot from Venice's many
expeditions and conquests, brought back
and added to the building.

The Golden Age

The huge 17th century church of Santa Maria della Salute dominates the entrance to the Grand Canal on the approach from St. Mark's Square. It was built following a terrible plague which had threatened to wipe out Venice. During the plague the city authorities vowed to build a church so that God would be merciful and allow Venice to survive. The following year the plague subsided and Venice kept its promise—Basilica della Salute took nearly 50 years to build.

The Golden Age

As the fourteenth and fifteenth centuries progressed, the strongest power in the Mediterranean was the growing Ottoman Empire. Constantinople fell to the Turks in 1453 and became the powerful center of the Ottoman Empire, with trading and political arms radiating out across the entire Near East and most of the Mediterranean Sea. However, although Venice lost Negroponte to the Ottomans in 1470, the Republic remained a significant presence around the eastern Mediterranean, even taking Cyprus in 1489 (they retained possession until 1573). As two voracious trading rivals, Venice and the Ottomans frequently came to blows, with the Venetians claiming the justification of acting in the interests of the defense of Christianity against the Infidel. The Ottoman Empire proceeded to chip away at Venetian and other European areas of interest by taking the islands of Rhodes in 1522, Chios in 1566, and Cyprus in July 1570. Malta withstood a prolonged siege in 1565.

In the late 14th century Milan rose to prominence as a trading rival at the same time as Venetian maritime trade was suffering thanks to the actions of the Turks. So, to protect the vital trade routes into northern Europe and safeguard mainland property investments, the Republic was forced out of her chosen isolation into forming an uneasy alliance with her old enemy Florence, fired in a common interest in keeping the Milanese out of northern Italy. Furthermore, Venetian power started to decline as commercial prosperity slowly but inexorably shifted from the Mediterranean to the Atlantic and away from Venice's sphere of influence. The Atlantic maritime nations of Portugal, England, and the Netherlands were starting to shift the emphasis of trade in their direction. Venice reluctantly acknowleged this commercial reality by moving its wealth into local industry and Italian mainland agricultural property.

In 1404, for the first time, Venice decided to extend into mainland Italy and within two decades had annexed Padua, Vicenza, Verona, Belluna, Feltre, and Friuli. In order to control her new dominions the Venetian government

LEFT: Until the 19th century the only bridge over the Grand Canal was the famous Rialto Bridge—since then two more have been constructed.

divided itself into two parts: the stato da mar (the colonial sea state) and the stato da terra (the land state). Soon Venice controlled lands across the Po Valley and as far as the River Adda.

By the late 15th century Venice was so powerful on the Italian mainland and such a threat that Milan, Florence, and Naples allied together against the Republic. During the same period (1494) France invaded Italy and Venice took advantage of the distraction to try to take the port of Apuila and to annex Pisa. Then, in a step too far, Venice attempted to take the Papal territory of Romagna. Pope Julius II was furious and in 1508 at the Treaty of Cambrai forged an alliance called the League of Cambrai of all the other Italian city-states plus a number of European monarchies against the Republic of Venice. On May 14, 1509, at the Battle of Agnadello the mercenary-dominated Republic army was routed by the French and over 4,000 of her forces died. Most of her mainland territory was occupied by either French or Imperial forces causing the other Venetian-held territories to revolt. Venice was on the brink of collapse.

Disaster was unwittingly averted by Pope Julius II who changed sides against the French as soon as he got what he wanted (Romagna), not that he cared about Venice; instead he became even deeper embroiled in the ancient bitter rivalries between the Papacy, France (Francis I), Spain (Ferdinand and Isabella), and the Holy Roman Emperor (Charles V). This left Venice with the opportunity to retake virtually all her lost possessions, at which point she announced her armed neutrality and intention not to get involved in European conflicts.

During the Renaissance Venice blossomed as a great center of the arts with such homegrown luminaries as Giovanni and Gentile Bellini, Titian, Carpaccio, Veronese, Giorgione, and Tintoretto. The arts scene was vibrant and the architecture magnificent. But her trading empire started to shrink from the beginning of the 16th century with the Ottoman Empire moving into traditional Venetian trading centers around the Aegean and eastern Mediterranean. Even in their Adriatic home waters the Turk harried Venetian

LEFT: A panorama of the Grand Canal with the Rialto Bridge at extreme right, photographed c. 1908. The Grand Canal is the vestigial river bed of the Brenta River which for centuries has been an important transport route. Wealthy Venetian merchants built their homes alongside the watercourse and so the Grand Canal developed as the heart of Venice.

BELOW: The Rialto Bridge c. 1890. The first bridge was made of wood with a central opening section but was rebuilt in stone between 1588 and 1591. The design was the subject of intense argument between rival architects including Palladio and Michelangelo, but the competition was won by Antonio da Ponte.

traders and shipping and the effects were felt in the coffers back in Venice. The government suffered as a consequence and was forced to raise unpopular taxes on their merchants.

BELOW: The Bocca di Leone (letterbox) on the Doge's Palace was used to report crimes anonymously, this one was used to denounce tax evaders.

RIGHT: The Church of the Scalzi, next to

the bridge of the same name, was the only building in the area to survive the construction of the station.

FAR RIGHT: Venice is lit up at night to show off the beauty of the architecture.

LEFT AND FAR LEFT: Venice is full of fabulous churches, almost all built in magnificent style. By the 18th century there were over 200 churches in the city, some of them built by the state, some built by wealthy religious orders, and some by wealthy, pious families. All of them are worth a visit. At left, the Basilica of Santa Maria della Salute, a great octagonal edifice surmounted by two domes and covered in Istrian stone.

ABOVE: The church on Isola San Michele, the Isle of the Dead, was built in Istrian stone in the 1460s.

Carnevale di Venezia

Venice observes good Roman Catholic tradition except at carnival time when the mood completely changes. In the old days the Carnival started on December 26, S. Stefano Day, and lasted as a running party until the break of Ash Wednesday and the beginning of Lent. The Carnival probably has its roots in the Repubblica della Serenissima's (the Most Serene Republic of Venice) victory against Ulrico, Patriarch of Aquileia, in the year 1162, when to celebrate the event dances and games started to take place in the Piazza San Marco (St. Mark's Square) and the slaughter of 12 pigs and a bull.

The first record of Carnival is a document dated May 2, 1268, which forbids the game of the "eggs," presumably a riotous and damaging debacle. However, it seems that Venetians took little or no notice of official disapproval and a series of laws had to be passed over the years to try to control the behavior of revelers and stop the rot of general moral decline. A decree of 1339 prohibited masqueraders from carousing around the city at night, and many laws were passed forbidding the carrying or arms and weapons of all descriptions; various musical instruments—especially drums—had to remain silent until midday.

All the main piazzas and thoroughfares were thronged with people singing and dancing, playing riotous games and flirting with the opposite sex. All rules were off and licentious behavior was no longer shocking (except to the clergy, many of whom no doubt joined in). It was forbidden to wear religious clothes with a mask and masked people were not allowed to enter any of the holy places, such as nunneries and churches.

On Shrove Tuesday, the last day of Carnival, an effigy of the Carnival was burned on St. Mark's Square and the end of Carnival was signalled at midnight by the tolling of the bells of San Francesco della Vigna. Masks and costumes were put away and once the hangovers had cleared order, calm, and presidence resumed. Venice could get back to the serious business of commerce.

The ancient Carnival had its heyday in the 18th century but declined in line with Venice's power and importance. In 1797 Napoleon signed the Treaty of

Campo Formio giving Venice to the Austrian Kingdom of Lombardy. The Austrians moved in on January 18, 1798 and the Carnival went into decline. The Austrians strongly disapproved of the long period of anarchy and debauchery entailed by the Carnival and actively discouraged the festivities. Finally the Carnival was banned altogether by Mussolini in the 1930s and not revived until 1979. The modern Venice Carnival is a much less riotous affair and has become a massive annual tourist attraction with organized events and parades.

LEFT AND PREVIOUS PAGE: Carnival was revived in 1979 by the city and has proved a huge visitor attraction. In 1994 about 45,000 people came to see the fun and every year the figure has increased, by 2002 it was attracting 800,000 people. It is now almost too popular.

ABOVE: A typical canal scene.

RIGHT: On the Grand Canal Palazzo Giustinian (now the Glass Museum) sits next to the Gothic palace of Ca' Foscari (far right), now the seat of Venice University. Ca' Foscari was built for Doge Francesco Foscari. Many distinguished visitors have stayed there, including Henri III of France in 1574.

PAGE 58: Ca' Pesaro was built by a rich merchant family at the end of the 15th century (begun in 1652, finished in 1710) in Venetian Baroque style. It has twice since changed hands, firstly to become Palazzo Degli Orfei, and then at the end of the 19th century it became Palazzo Fortuny, the home of the famous fabric designer and painter Mariano Fortuny. In 1956 his widow left the palazzo to the city of Venice.

PAGE 59: Construction started on Ca' Rezzonico in 1667 but financial constraints left the building unfinished for over 70 years. In 1751 it was sold to the Rezzonico family who completed the building in lavish style. After changing hands it was bought by the Italian state in 1934 and became a museum.

RIGHT: Palazzo Vendramin-Calergi has been described as the finest example of Tuscan Renaissance architecture in Venice. It was built at the end of the 16th century for the fabulously wealthy Loredan family but later passed through many owners. The composer Richard Wagner died here in 1883. In 1946 it was bought by the city of Venice and turned into a winter casino.

FAR RIGHT: Not all the houses in Venice are as grand as the palaces, but they are still completely lovely in their own more modest way.

PAGE 62: View down the Grand Canal towards the station, with the Church of St. Geremia to the right of the photograph and the Church of the Scalzi central.

PAGE 63: Empty gondolas waiting for tourists.

RIGHT: Recent archaeological investigations have shown that Venice has been sinking much faster and for much longer than anyone previously realized or has been documented. The proof for this has been found all over the city where layer upon layer of pavements and foundations have been laid on top of each other over the centuries in a continuous battle to keep the Venice above the waters of the Lagoon.

ABOVE: A statue on the facade of St. Mark's Basilica.

OPPOSITE PAGE, LEFT AND RIGHT: Statues lining the veranda leading to the entrance of the first floor of the Doge's Palace.

RIGHT: One of the two statues by Jacopo Sansovino flanking the Scala dei Giganti (Giants Staircase) in the courtyard of the Doge's Palace. The statues of Mars and Neptune symbolize Venice's authority over land and sea.

RIGHT: Looking across St. Mark's Basin at San Giorgio Maggiore. This great church is Andrea Palladio's masterpiece and was built between 1565 and 1559 during the Golden Age of Venice. Every St. Stephen's Day (December 26) the Doge would come here to celebrate Mass sung by a double choir made up from St. Mark's choristers and the Benedictine monks from the nearby monastery.

FAR RIGHT: Behind San Giorgio towers the Campanile San Marco. The bell tower belongs to St. Mark's Basilica and is located in the piazza of the same name. The first tower on this site was a watch tower for the early docks built in the 8th century. Then a succession of ever larger towers were built on the site over the centuries. The campanile looks today as it did on its completion in 1514, however the first incarnation of this tower collapsed in 1902 and this is the 1912 reconstruction.

Decline and end of the Republic

A canal on the island of Murano.

Decline and end of the Republic

In 1618 the Thirty Years War started, embroiling much of Europe in conflict. Although not directly involved general trading suffered and by 1620 Venice was in the throes of economic crisis. To make matters worse a great plague swept across northern Italy in 1630, an event now linked to the beginning of the decline of Venice. As a thriving port Venice was particularly badly hit and unfortunately contemporary doctors and scientists did not make the connection between the rats and the plague, so the ships continued to bring in the deadly pestilence. In just 17 months 80,000 people died in the Republic, including the Doge Nicolò Contarini, as well as many important governing figures and merchants, depriving Venice of much of her political cunning and experience. As a whole it has been estimated that northern Italy and Tuscany lost nearly seventy percent of its population to the plague.

An important side effect of the devastation was the depletion of soldiers and fighting men leaving Venetian overseas territories and valuable shipping routes poorly protected. In 1645 the War of Candia started when the Turks attempted to take Crete, which they finally achieved in 1669. This costly war is estimated to have tallied the loss of around 108,000 Turks and 29,088 "Christians" (mostly Venetians, Greeks, and French volunteers). Despite the following peace treaty the struggle continued, bleeding dry Venetian lives and the once unimaginably wealthy Venetian coffers. Such continuous battles plus the ravages of the plague greatly diminished Venice's fighting prowess and its ability to protect its merchants—the very bringers of wealth to the Republic. Overall Venice had become a much-weakened Republic and a shadow of its former self.

The Turks followed up with victory in 1714 at Morea (the old name for the Peloponnese peninsula in southern Greece). Interestingly, at this period in

ABOVE: Many of the buildings in Venice are in dire need of attention, but the price is increasingly costly in such an environmentally challenging city.

RIGHT: Map of Venice dating from 1886, about 20 years after Venice and the Veneto had become a part of Italy following the defeat Austria at the Battle of Königgrät.

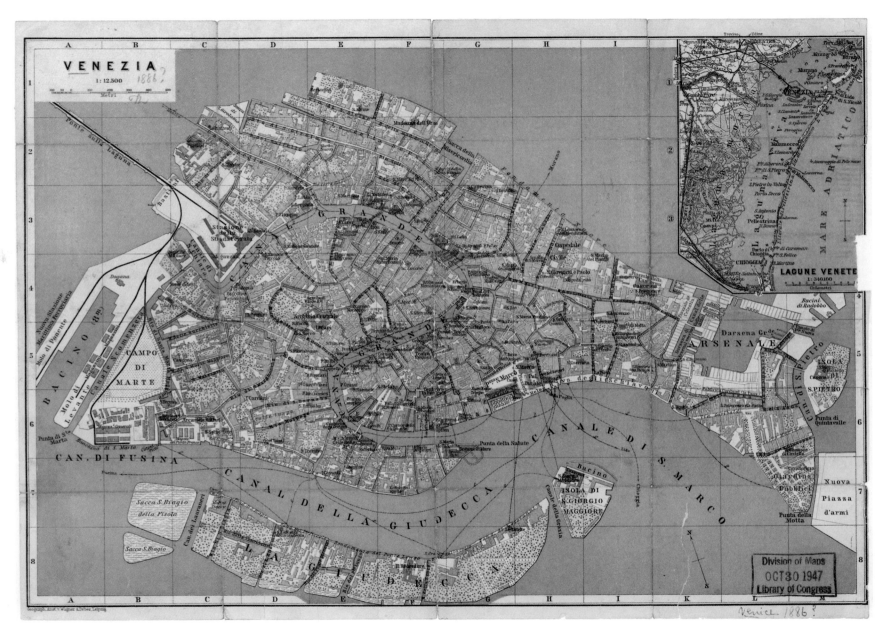

VENEZIA

1:12.500

CANAL GRANDE

CANAL DELLA GIUDECCA

CANALE DI S. MARCO

history, the Ottoman Turks did not suffer from the plague and so were able to take exceptional advantage over the stricken Italian city-states such as Venice. Meanwhile other traders started to avoid dealing with Venetians for fear of catching the plague. Sudden inflation fanned the Venetian economy, trade almost ceased so the price of goods and produce rocketed and rich and poor alike suffered as a consequence. Trade declined and the luxury industries were no longer required.

End of the Republic

In 1714 with the loss of Morea, Venetian military and naval power disappeared altogether and Venice was left with a legacy of magnificent churches, beautiful palaces, and wonderful art treasures as reminders of former glories. In 1792 Napoleon and France were attempting to dominate Europe and in terrified response the rest of Europe created a coalition against the French. The exception was Venice, which in the shape of the Grand Council led by Doge Ludovico Manin, decided it was in the Republic's best interests to remain neutral, hoping that events would by-pass them. Ignoring this intent Napoleon offered Venice a full alliance in 1796, but Venice clung to her stated neutrality, even though both French and Austrian troops crossed her territories at will.

On January 14, 1794, Napoleon beat the Austrians at the Battle of Rivoli: for the following peace Napoleon wanted the Austrians to abandon the left bank of the Rhine, so he offered them Venice in exchange. Furious Venetians attacked French troops in the Veneto in spring 1797, and an equally livid Napoleon refused to accept the Venetian Senate's apologies and instead demanded a change in the Republic's constitution and marched his troops on Venice. Fearing the imminent arrival of the French the Doge and Council resigned on May 12 while outside the public panicked. Four days later a peoples' municipality was chosen and a committee of public safety elected. The new government meekly requested that Napoleon's troops occupy Venice, meanwhile Austria seized the Venetian territories of Istria and Dalmatia.

On May 12, 1797 Napoleon delivered the "Pasque Veronesi" (the Veronese Easters), which abolished the Venetian constitution. Then, on October 17, 1797 by the Treaty of Campoformio and without consultation or compensa-

tion, Venice lost its 1,070 years of Republican government and independence when it was handed over to the Austrians. Before they left, however, the French helped themselves to as much of Venice's wealth as they could carry away, including valuable manuscripts, paintings, and most notably the four magnificent gilded horse statues of St.Mark, themselves looted from Byzantium. French soldiers vandalised all the images of St.Mark and as a deliberate final insult, the bucintoro—the Doge's ceremonial barge—was burned. The gilded horses were taken to Paris and displayed in the Tuileries. On January 18, 1798, Austrian troops entered Venice to general public acclaim, so much did the Venetians hate and fear the French.

Following Napoleon's victory at Austerlitz and the Treaty of Presbourg in December 26, 1805, Venice and the Veneto were incorporated into the Kingdom of Italy. However, France returned the following year and retook Venice in January 1806. After a period of occupation the Austrians threw out the French in April 1814 and made Venice a free port. Most of the looted works of art, including the horses, were returned from France in 1815.

Nevertheless Venice's glory days were long gone and the city's decline continued, especially between 1830 and 1848 when the Austrians were thrown out for a short time before returning to lay siege to Venice in 1849. In August the provisional Venetian government fell and the Austrians returned yet again, this time removing all Venice's administrative powers over the Veneto. Austrian rule was severe and the city suffered accordingly. Relief came at last in 1866 when Venice officially became a part of Italy under a new Italian monarch. Venice and the Veneto were given to the king as a reward for supporting Prussia after the defeat of the Austrian forces at the Battle of Königgräz (aka Battle of Sadowa), the final and decisive battle of the Austro-Prussian War.

FAR LEFT: Late 19th century view of a typical Venetian campi. Fresh water was drawn from wells attached to deep underwater cisterns that collected rainwater.

LEFT: The predominant colors of Venice are drawn from a rich Renaissance blend of subtle reds, terra cotta, rose, and yellows, all merging beautifully together.

ABOVE: The view from the campanile in the late 19th century towards S. Maria della Salute. Note the sailing ships in the Lagoon.

RIGHT: A later view of Venice harbor now providing shelter for steam ships.

ABOVE: The first Venetian guidebook for tourists was published in 1581 and despite its fine architecture and cultural attractions the city soon gained a reputation for catering to "exotic" tastes, earning itself the reputation of being the "fleshpot of Europe."

RIGHT: As Venetian trade declined new prosperity started to grow through the growth of the tourist industry, in the early years of which most visitors arrived by sea on one of the many steamers that plied the Mediterranean.

6877. P. Z. - VENEZIA

now in ruin and St. Marks Cathedral Venice Italy

ABOVE, RIGHT, AND FAR RIGHT: St. Mark's Campanile was designed by Sansovino, completed in 1549, and then extended in 1663. The tower contains five bells and is capped by a pyramid then topped by a weathervane in the form of a golden angel. Suddenly, on July 14, 1902, the campanile collapsed, in the process demolishing the logetta; amazingly, the only fatality was the caretaker's cat. The city authorities decided to rebuild the campanile exactly as it looked before, but with the precaution of internal reinforcements. The campanile was officially reopened on April 25, St. Mark's Day, 1912.

ABOVE: A sketch showing the rebuilding of the Campanile dated 1911.

RIGHT: Amateur and professional artists alike flocked to Venice to paint the city, flooding the art market with romantic views.

FAR RIGHT: Gondoliers outside Simeone Piccolo. Designed by Giovanni Scalfarotto on the upper reaches of the Grand Canal, this church is an 18th century imitation of the Pantheon in Rome. It is now used as a concert venue.

ABOVE: A late 19th century tinted photograph of a gondola on the Grand Canal. These days the canal would be crammed with river traffic and anything but peaceful.

RIGHT: Another view of the Punta della Dogana, or Customs Point. The tower of the building is topped by twin Atlases holding up a bronze globe. On top of the globe itself is a statue of Fortuna (Fortune) which acts as a weathervane.

ABOVE AND RIGHT: At the turn of the 19th century Venice was slowly starting to recover from economic depression. Then the historic isolation of the city was changed forever in 1846 when a railroad bridge was constructed and more visitors could flock in. From this time onwards tourism has steadily grown to become vital to Venice's economy.

FAR RIGHT: A military parade in St. Mark's Square.

PAGES 92 AND 93: The numerous campanile of Venice are usually tall, square towers topped with an open chamber containing the bells above which is either a pyramid top or an onion-shaped dome. Due to their unstable foundations the campanile are in a constant state of repair and in danger of total collapse.

ABOVE: A sketch of Venice from across the Lagoon by James McNeill Whistler (1834–1903). In 1879 Whistler had declared himself bankrupt following a damaging court case in London and fled to Venice where he joined his mistress. However, the London Fine Art Society helped him by funding and commissioning work from him which resulted in over 90 pastels and 50 etchings. With his improved financial position Whistler was able to return to London the following year. His new efforts were published between 1880 and 1886, they were widely exhibited and proved greatly influential on many artists.

Masqueraders

It was the practice for masqueraders to enter the cities nunneries and chat to the nuns, but another law dated January 24, 1458 shows that things went much further. This decree forbade men from entering the city's convents dressed as women and committing "multas inhonestates." Masqueraders were forbidden from entering churches and the common people were similarly not allowed to enter wearing indecent attire. The license granted by the wearing of a mask—traditionally made of papier-mâché—and the consequent immoral behaviour meant that some people took to wearing a mask all year round; this was stopped on August 13, 1608 when the city Serenissima (Council of Ten) declared that the wearing of masks was threatening the stability and reputation of Venice and from then on was only permissible during carnival and at official banquets. Punishment for men could be two years in jail, 18 months rowing while ankle-chained in one of the Republic's galleys, and a 500 lire fine payable to the Council. For women the penalty was a public whipping from St.Mark's to the Rialto and then chained up between two columns for the public to abuse. Following this they were banished from Venetian territory for four years and fined 500 lire.

In 1703 masks were banned all year round from gambling clubs because debtors were avoiding their creditors too easily.

Carnival started with a series of official balls and theatrical performances followed by spontaneous parties. Revellers donned masks and fanciful costumes, the more elaborate the better. The most traditional costume consisted of a voluminous black cloak, round glasses, and a long-nosed mask—this is the plague-doctor, the beak echoes his long breathing apparatus that held a sponge doused in vinegar, thought to hold the plague at bay. The doctor also traditionally carries a long cane or stick to touch the sick with and avoid direct contact with the disease. But ladies, in particular, demanded more elaborate and exquisite masks.

As early as the 15th century the mascherari (mask makers) had their own official artisan status because their work was so important to the carnival.

Masks gave valuable anonymity—particularly to the nobility who normally lived in a regime of strict precedence and regulation—the freedom to mix with the common people at the theater, in the squares, gambling rooms, in fact all around the city and to move with complete ease among the crowds. Their sinister appearance only seemed to add to the appeal.

BELOW AND RIGHT: The masquerade allowed too much license for bad behavior and many laws were passed to curb and control the revellers. The modern masqueraders are much better behaved than their earlier forebears.

THESE PAGES: There are about 400 bridges around Venice, the most famous of which is the Bridge of Sighs (Right) that joins the Doge's Palace (Palazzo Ducale) and the old Republic's prison. Most Venetian bridges have a single semicircular arch. Originally made of wood, to make them permanent the canal had to be almost emptied so that foundations could be sunk on either side and a wooden mold constructed for the stone and brickwork.

Modern Venice

Modern Venice

With her absorption into Italy Venice was able to throw off the chains of foreign oppression and enter the modern world properly. The city's geographical isolation had been already breached by the construction of a railroad bridge in 1846 that joined the city with mainland Italy; although a road bridge was not completed until 1932. Attempts to revive Venice as an important trading center foundered, even when the industrial zone was started at Mestre and the Lagoon started to be exploited and a popular seaside resort was developed at the Lido. After World War II the economy of Venice underwent attempts at revival but with no success, for numerous reasons Venice was unable to join in the general northern Italian economic prosperity.

These reasons had to do with Venice's relative geographical isolation at the far end of the Adriatic, the traditional luxury industries had suffered greatly during the wars, the indigenous population was abandoning Venice for jobs and a better standard of living in other north Italian cities—particularly to Mestre and Marghera—and the price of property was already becoming too expensive for ordinary Venetians. Pollution and heavy canal traffic was taking an increasingly obvious toll on the city and the acque alte was occurring more frequently.

Today Venice is declining in population faster than it is growing, and at least a quarter of Venetians are over the age of 65. Many wealthy second-

PAGE 98–99: View across the Lagoon at sunset.

RIGHT: Many visitors arrive in Venice on board huge luxury cruise liners that dwarf the old city with their out-scaled size. Venice is one of the most popular tourist destinations in the world attracting over fourteen million visitors a year and rising to a city with a dwindling native population of around 65,000 and dropping; at the end of the 19th century the population of Venice was between 130,000 and 150,000 people.

homers are buying in Venice, but native Venetians are becoming harder to find as traditional jobs in the old industries and luxury businesses disappear under the weight of cheaper foreign alternatives. The danger is that Venice will become a large theme park whose only inhabitants are tourists, part-time home owners, and people directly involved in the tourist trade. The price of houses has soared putting the prospect of owning a property well out of the reach of all but the wealthiest locals.

The great flood of 1966

The most important event in recent Venetian history happened suddenly in 1966 when a great muddy tidal surge inundated the city endangering every-thing that was Venice and showing just how fragile and vulnerable this extraor-dinarily beautiful but sinking city had become. Until1966 it was an accepted fact that Venice was in danger but nobody was doing anything about it, there was a lot of discussion and a great deal of argument but seemingly little urgency.

The great flood changed all that: the arguing continued but with a new urgency, the waters, if nothing else, brought the attention of the entire world to the perilous state that Venice had fallen to and the city's imminent collapse. At the beginning of November 1966 unusually heavy rains fell over northern and central Italy and by the night of the 2nd villagers living high up the Arno val-ley started calling the emergency services for help. In just two days a third of the region's annual rainfall had fallen and the river levels were rising dangerously all across northern Italy. The floodwaters devastated the ancient city of Florence and damaged villages and towns all over central and north Italy. In Venice the floodwaters went on to inundate the city on November 4 brought in over the Lagoon on an unusually high tidal surge.

The muddy and saline Lagoon waters stayed in the city for fifteen long hours before retreating. Even so, Venice was cut off from the outside world for 24 hours as the floodwaters swirled around the canals. Storm drains erupted with salty lagoon water pouring silt and muddy water across the historic piaz-zas. In the historic heart of Venice the average waters reached over 19 inches deep and in St. Mark's Square the waters were 4 feet deep. Despite this Venetians did have a slither of luck, had the flood waters hit the city five hours

earlier, it would have coincided with high tide and the waters would have risen to around 8 feet above normal sea level which really would have destroyed many historic sites.

The muddy flood waters filled basements and shops alike and over seventy-five percent of Venetian businesses, shops, and artisans' studios were seriously damaged, not to mention the thousands of goods that were completely ruined or destroyed. The impact on Venice's historic buildings was catastrophic and in many cases hastened an existing decay problem to crisis point. The ground floors of the canalside buildings flooded and many of them—an estimated 16,000 houses—have in effect been abandoned ever since. Amazingly nobody died, but thousands of people were trapped in their homes and more than 1,200 residents had to abandon their houses and on the island of Pellestrina 2,000 people had to flee to higher ground. Many of these people have never returned to live in their native city and statistics show that Venice has lost half its population since 1966. The register of residents which is compiled every ten years show that the population of Venice proper has almost halved since 1966 from 121,000 to 62,000 souls.

Italian National Council for Research claims that these days with much more sensitive and sophisticated weather forecasting six days warning of impending flood could have been issued. Ever since the 1966 flood debate has raged in Venice and around the world as to the best way to protect this unique city. After decades of assessments and studies the Italian government finally agreed a $3 billion project to fund the building of 79 huge hinged barriers to separate Venice and the lagoon from the rising waters of the Adriatic. The gates will protect Venice from a six-foot tidal surge and should keep the sea at bay for at least 70 years. The project is hugely controversial, especially among environmentalists.

LEFT: At the western entrance to the Grand Canal lies the quarter known as Cannaregio—the station quarter—and the Bridge of the Scalzi. Built in 1934 it replaced a 19th century iron bridge and links the Church of the Scalzi to the other bank.

RIGHT AND FAR RIGHT: Venetian shops are small and enchanting and full of deliciously tempting objects, many of them locally made. Venetian specialities include glass—especially glass beads and magnificent chandeliers—lacemaking, marbled paper, masks, and miniature gondolas. Additionally, of course, there are lots of different local speciality foods and candies.

LEFT AND ABOVE: Gondoliers stand upright in the bows of their gondolas and, unusually, face the direction in which they are proceeding. The gondolier rows by pushing his single oar forwards and using it also as a rudder to steer.

FAR LEFT: Poster advertising the attractions of Venice.

LEFT: The winged lion of Venice and St. Mark stands against the background of a starry night sky at the top of the Torre Dell 'Orogolio clock tower above the clock face. Above this stand a pair of bronze automata figures called "The Moors" who strike the bell on the hour.

FAR LEFT: Sculpture of Doge Francesco Foscari (1423–57) and the lion of St. Mark on the front of the Doge's Palace. The original sculpture was destroyed in 1797 and remade by Luigi Ferrari in 1885.

ABOVE, RIGHT AND PAGES 114–115:
A selection of mouthwatering Venetian
temptations including pastries,
icecream, fruit and vegetables.

RIGHT: Most Venetians and tourists use the ubiquitous vaporettos for moving around the city: they are much quicker and infinitely cheaper than the beautiful gondolas. The easiest and most economical way to move around Venice is by waterbus of which there are two types: the large vaporetti work the busiest routes and make frequent stops to let people on and off; and the motoscafi which are smaller and much faster. In addition there are expensive water taxis and the very expensive and leisurely gondolas.

FAR RIGHT: Vaporettos working in the evening sunlight.

LEFT AND BELOW: The oldest parts of the city are divided into six areas called sestieri—these are Castello, Cannaregio, San Polo, Dorsoduro, Santa Croce, and San Marco. The calli, campi, and campielli—lane, squares, and small squares—have unusual names that reflect very localized events in Venice. Sometimes they are historic taken from the jobs or names of the people who lived there, or perhaps from some incident that happened on that very spot. Street names appear on the outside of buildings written on small white squares called *nizioleti* (see below) that translates as "towels."

LEFT AND FAR LEFT: Venice is a city that rarely sleeps, there is always another festival to look forward to. For instance, the Carnivale lasts for ten days up to Lent on Shrove Tuesday and culminates in a masked ball. During May the feast of La Sensa takes place on the first Sunday after Ascension. La Festa del Redentore celebrates and commemorates the end of the plague in 1576, for this a bridge of boats is constructed across the canal so that the faithful can walk across the waters and then enjoy the huge firework display. Another fun event is the Regata Storica on the first Sunday in September, when the gondoliers compete against each other in trials of skill and strength. During fall, in late August and early September, the fabulous Venice Film Festival takes place on the Lido. Then, every other year since 1895, the Venice Biennale has been held to celebrate modern art.

PAGES 120–121: Venice is a city of canals, somewhere in the region of 150 of them. These canals are filled with saline waters from the Lagoon as well as an annual rainfall of 34 inches. In July the temperature averages a comfortable 75°F, but can get oppressively hot and sticky in August, while in January the average is 36°F. The best weather is often between March and May.

THESE PAGES: Glass making has been a Venetian industry since the late 10th century and a particular specialization of the island of Murano since the 13th century when all the glass manufacturers' of Venice were asked to move there to remove the risk of fire from their furnaces igniting the city. For 200 years (between the 15th and 17th centuries) Murano was the biggest and most important supplier of glass in Europe. The tourist industry is now the most important source of income for Murano glassmakers.

PAGE 124: Everything in Venice has to be moved over water.

PAGE 125: The water ambulance is one of the few vessels permitted to move at speed along the old waterways. But sometimes when the water is high the boat cannot get under a number of the bridges. This is also a problem for the fire and police services as well as ordinary boats.

LEFT AND FAR LEFT: Despite the tourists ordinary Venetians go about their daily business as usual. The markets are great meeting places where food and gossip are equally important.

PAGES 128–129: Most people who come to Venice just come for the day, only a very small percentage actually stay in the city. So the best time to really see Venice is in the evenings when the majority of the tourists have left and the canal sides are much quieter and more romantic.

ABOVE, RIGHT, AND PAGES 132–133: The
balconies of Venice are a fine vantage point
from which to admire the city.

LEFT: The many campi (or public squares) have been at the center of Venetian local life where adults relaxed, children played, and traders bought and sold goods.

ABOVE: This bronze door knocker in the form of a grotesque head is typically Venetian, other popular local forms include lion's heads and clowns.

PAGES 136–137, AND LEFT: During the tourist season in the summer and fall months all the restaurants are open, the hotels full, and the canals throng with people and excitement. But the evenings are quieter as many of the visitors only come into Venice for the day as they are staying elsewhere, so leaving Venice much quieter and more relaxed.

RIGHT AND FAR RIGHT: Many of the buildings lining the back canals are in poor condition and desperately in need of repair and attention. Even so, the cost of housing in Venice is way beyond the pocket of many native Venetians who are forced through economic circumstances to leave their homes for better paid and more secure jobs on the mainland. Much of Venice is now owned by foreigners, the only people who can afford the housing, but many of them are second homers who do not spend a great deal of time or money in Venice. Venice is in the grip of a quiet crisis: it is slowly becoming inundated by the waters of the Adriatic and depopulated fueled by the lack of jobs for the locals.

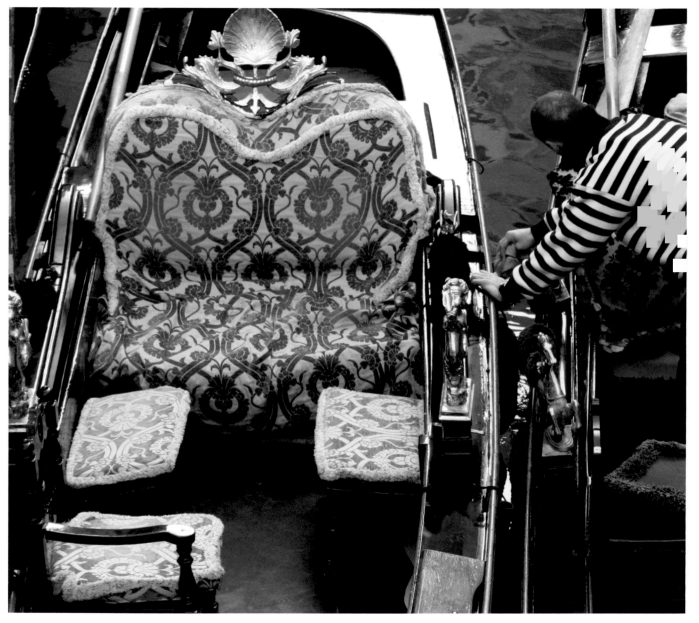

PAGES 142–145: One of the unmissable sights of Venice are the gondoliers and their opulent boats. Locally cast brass trevisan or seahorses are traditionally used to embellish the sides of gondolas. Gondolas are black because in the past the nobles became so competitive about decorating their boats ever more lavishly that it became so ridiculous that the city authorities passed a law that they all must be painted black.

ABOVE AND RIGHT: A trip in a gondolier can be one of the most romantic Venetian experiences, especially on a warm summer evening through the quieter backwaters of the city. The profession of gondolier has been passed from father to son down the generations. These days gondoliers wear black pants with stripped tops complete with a red or blue ribboned straw hat (in sunny weather). In past times the gondoliers wore much gaudier clothing and their boats were brightly painted, but this was stopped by law in 1633. The boat itself is constructed so that one of its sides is 9in broader than the other which means that the gondolier naturally inclines to the right (or starboard). This tendency is corrected by the gondolier standing at the stern using his single oar to correct his course. These days there are about 400 gondoliers in Venice who earn their living from the tourist trade.

ABOVE: The Venetian police use fast
motorboats to go about their business.

RIGHT: To get off the beaten track
inevitably requires a sightseeing boat trip.

RIGHT: The island of the Lido is eight miles long and acts as a barrier between the Lagoon and the Adriatic Sea. It is a popular destination for tourists and Venetians alike and has attracted many great writers such as Thomas Mann and the poet Lord Byron. The beach at the Lido is a very lovely spot and has been often shown on film, most memorably in Mann's novel *Death in Venice*.

CENTER LEFT: A poster advertising Venice and its Lido.

LEFT: The Lido's Hotel des Bains.

ABOVE AND RIGHT: Glance down the narrower back streets away from the main tourist sites and chances are that there will be Venetian men sitting around, reading the newspaper, and chatting over a glass of local wine as they catch up with all the latest gossip and soccer scores.

FAR RIGHT: There are no cars in Venice so when any goods leave the water they have to be carried—inevitably up and down steep steps and narrow alleyways.

FAR LEFT: A gondola yard in the San Trovaso, one of the lesser visited areas of Venice so much quieter and relaxed than in the center of the city with all its tourists and restaurants.

LEFT: This front-facing view of a gondola clearly shows the asymmetrical shape of this unique craft that the gondolier works hard to counteract.

RIGHT: The Grand Canal is around two miles long and contains an astonishing number of beautiful palaces—over 200 of them. At night the "Canalazzo" is one of the most beautiful sights in the world.

LEFT: The Doge's Palace and St. Mark's Square in the quiet of the early hours.

Acque alte, 10, 11
Adda, river, 48
Adriatic, 8, 10, 20, 23, 24, 27, 28, 48, 100, 140, 150
Agnadello, Battle of, 48
Alexander III, Pope, 24, 74
Apuila, 48
Aquileia, 23, 54
Arsenal, 22, 23
Aslexius, 24
Attila the Hun, 20

Barbarosa, Frederick, 24, 74
Bari, 28
Bellini, Giovanni and Gentile, 48
Belluna, 28, 26
Bergamo, 28
Black Death/plague, 27, 72, 74
Bocca di Leone, 50
Bonaparte, Napoleon, 8, 54, 56, 74-77
Boniface of Montferrat, 24
Bora wind, 10
Brenta, river, 8, 23, 48-49
Brescia, 28
Bridge of Sighs, 96
Brindisi, 28
Buon, Giovanni, 31
Burano, 20
Byron, Lord, 150
Byzantine empire, 23, 26
Byzantium, 20, 23, 26, 35, 77
Byzantium, sack of, 24, 35

Ca' Foscari, 57
Ca' Pesaro, 58
Ca' Rezzonico, 59
Campanile San Marco, 69, 82-83, 84
Campanile, 4, 90, 91
Campoformio, Treaty of, 74, 75
Carnivale di Venezia, 54-57, 94-95, 119
Carpaccio, 48
Charlemagne, 20
China, 27
Chioggia, 27
Chios, 46

Church of the Scalzi, 50, 62
Cicladi, 28
Clocks, 30, 36
Constantinople, 38, 46
Contarini, Doge Nicolò, 72
Council of Sages, 38
Council of Ten, 38, 94
Cremona, 28
Crete, 72
Curzola, Battle of, 26
Cyprus, 46

Da Ponte, Antonio, 49
Dalmatia, 26, 27, 74
Dandolo, Admiral Andrea, 26
Dandolo, Doge Enrico, 24, 26, 35
Diocletian, 24
Dogana di Mare, 34, 35
Doge, 20, 36-39, 68, 77
Doge's Palace, 24, 31, 32, 33, 38, 39, 66. 67, 96, 108

Egypt, 24
Eubea, 28

Faenza, 28
Feltre, 28, 46
Ferrara, 27, 28
Ferrari, Luigi, 108, 109
Flag, 9
Florence, 46, 48, 102
Fondamenta Labia, 4
Foscari, Doge Francesco, 57, 108
Fourth Crusade, 24, 33
Franks, 20, 23
Friuli, 20, 46

Genoa, 24, 26, 27, 38
Giorgione, 48
Glass, 112-125
Gondola, 13, 14, 15, 63, 106-107, 142-145, 146, 147, 154, 155
Grand Canal, 4, 8, 16, 35, 46-47, 48-49, 57, 62-63, 64-65, 85, 86

Grand Tour, 8
Great Flood, 102, 104

Henri III, 57
Horses of St. Mark, 26, 35, 41, 42, 77

Innocent III, Pope, 24
Islam, 24
Isle of the Dead, 28, 29, 53
Istria, 74

Jerusalem, 24
Julius II, Pope, 48

Kingdom of Italy, 77
Königgräz, Battle of, 72, 77

La Giudecca, 31
La Serenissima, 9
Lagoon, 8, 10, 23, 27, 64, 78, 79, 80, 98-99, 100, 102, 119, 150
Latin Empire, 24
Levant, the, 26
Libra D'Oro, 38
Lido, 119, 150-151
Loggia dei Cavalli, 41, 42
Lombards, 20
Lombardy, 28, 56
Ludwig I, 27

Malamocco, 20
Malta, 46
Manin, Doge Ludovico, 74
Mann, Thomas, 150
Markets, 126-127
Mediterranean Sea, 23, 24, 26, 27, 46
Mercantile fleet, 20, 21, 24, 26
Merceria, 36
Merchants, 26, 33, 36, 48, 50
Mestre, 100
Michelangelo. 49
Milan, 27, 46, 48
Morea, 72, 74
Murano, 122-123
Mussolini, 56

Naples, 48
Negroponte, 46
Nizioleti, 117
Normans, 24
Orient, 24
Ottoman Empire, 27, 28, 46, 48

Padua, 27
Padua, 28, 46
Palaces, 13
Palazzo Fortuny, 58
Palazzo Giustinian, 57
Palazzo Vendramin-Calergi, 60
Palladio, Andrea, 49, 68-69
Pasque Veronesi, 74
Peace of Lodi, 28
Peace of Venice, 24, 74
Pepin, 20
Pisa, 24, 26, 48
Po, River, 8, 20, 28, 48
Polesine di Rovigo, 28
Police boats, 148
Polo, Marco, 26
Presbourg, Treaty of, 77
Punta della Dogana, 86

Quadriga — see Horses of St. Mark

Ravenna, 28
Renaissance, 8, 13, 48
Rhodes, 46
Rialto Bridge, 46-47, 48-49, 94, 118, 128
Rivo Alto, 23
Rivoli, Battle of, 74
Romagna, 48
Roman Empire, 20

Saint Geremia, 4, 64
San Francesco della Vigna, 54
San Giacomo di Rialto, 30, 31
San Giorgio Maggiore, 2, 68-69
San Michele monastery, 28, 29, 53
Sansovino, Jacopo, 66, 67
Santa Maria della Salute, 44-45,

52-53, 78
Serrata, 38
Shopping, 104-105, 110-113, 122-123, 126-127
Sicily, 24
Simeone Piccolo, 85
Sinking, 10, 12, 64, 102, 103
Sirocco wind, 10
St. Mark the Evangelist, 9, 14, 23, 77
St. Mark's Basilica, 23, 26, 40-41, 42-43, 66, 69
St. Mark's Basin, 2, 68-69
St. Mark's Square, 10, 17, 36, 54, 74-75, 89, 94, 102
Stato da mar, 48
Stato da terra, 48

Tetrarchs, 24, 25
Thirty Years' War, 72
Tintoretto, 48
Titian, 48
Torcello, 14, 20
Torre dell 'Orogolio, 109
Tourists, 38, 56, 80, 84, 100.101. 102, 114, 123, 127, 128, 129, 136-139
Treaty of Cambrai, 48
Trentino, 20
Treviso, 28
Turin, 27

Ulrico, Patriarch of Aquileia, 54
UNESCO World Heritage, 8

Vaporetto, 114, 115
Veneto, 20, 23, 77
Venice Biennale, 119
Verona, 28, 46
Veronese, 48
Vicenza, 28, 46
Wagner, Richard, 60
War of Candia, 72
Water ambulance, 125, 127
Whistler, James McNeill, 92-93
Winged lion, 12, 14, 23, 108-109
World War II, 100

Photo credits

Map page 9: Mark Franklin

Unless otherwise credited all photographs by **Gaz de Vere**.

Corbis

6 Wilfried Krecichwost/zefa; 18 Karl-Heinz Haenel/zefa; 21Sandro Vannini; 35 Mimmo Jodice; 42 (above right) Stapleton Collection; 44–45 Danny Lehman; 70–71 Eye Ubiquitous; 108 Danny Lehman; 109 Paul Seheult/Eye Ubiquitous

Hugh Alexander 10, 13, 54, 56, 61, 76 (right), 95, 98–99, 100, 107, 125, 126, 138, 144 (left), 145, 146, 150, 151 (right), 152, 153, 154, 155

Library of Congress Prints and Photographs Division 16, 22, 23, 25, 31, 37, 38, 39, 42 (above left), 48, 49, 58,59, 60, 73, 74, 76 (left), 78, 79, 80, 81, 82, 83, 84, 85, 86, 88, 89, 92, 96, 106, 151